Osprey AutoHistory

FERRARI 4-SEATERS

V12 Pininfarina 2+2; 1960 on

DAVID OWEN

Published in 1983 by Osprey Publishing Limited
12–14 Long Acre, London WC2 9LP
Member company of the George Philip Group

Sole distributors for the USA

Osceola, Wisconsin 54020, USA

British Library Cataloguing in Publication Data

Owen, David
    Ferrari four-seaters—(Autohistory)
    1. Ferrari automobile
    I. Title   II. Series
    629.2′222   TL215.F47
ISBN 0-85045-497-2

Editor Tim Parker
Associate Michael Sedgwick
Photography Mirco Decet
Design Trevor Vertigan

Filmset in Great Britain
Printed in Spain
by Grijelmo S. A., Bilbao.

Contents

Introduction

Of all the assignments which can face an auto-motive writer, turning out a book on Ferraris has to rate as one of the most enjoyable, and one of the most daunting. The enjoyment arises because, quite simply, it's a great deal more satisfying writing about cars which are either the very best, or the very worst, in the world. Extremes are always interesting, in a way in which cars which are functional rather than individual, efficient rather than interesting, mediocre rather than brilliant, could never hope to be—and there are no prizes for guessing which extremity of the scale of engineer-ing excellence provides space for the creations of *Commendatore* Enzo Ferrari. Given his experience, his obsessive determination and his ceaseless quest for mechanical and functional perfection, his cars are bound to earn respect from all enthusiasts everywhere, whatever the actual marque which sits at the top of their personal loyalty list.

And this is where the challenge comes in. Because so many people love Ferraris, worship them and study them with a fascination which borders on fanaticism, a yawning gap of potential errors opens up beneath the writer's faltering footsteps. An incorrect chassis number, a trifling mistake in a designation or a capacity measure-ment, or a slip in a styling detail, may escape detection in a work on a hitherto obscure and neglected make of motor car. Not so with Ferrari: anything which departs from the official record, or from the wealth of already published material on this most admired of stables, had better be justified, and backed up by authoritative and unimpeachable

sources, or the poor old writer will catch it in the neck from the automotive equivalent of 'Disgusted, Tunbridge Wells', writing in by the sackful to protest at any tampering with the Truth.

This, of course, is perfectly right and proper. But let me start with one important qualification. My previous AutoHistory, on the *Alfa Romeo Spiders*, was written from the view-point, not only of a committed enthusiast but also a driver who had owned one of the cars in question for almost a decade, and who had covered more than a hundred thousand miles behind the wheel. I have never, unfortunately, been lucky enough to own a Ferrari—nor to cover anything like a similar mileage at the controls of one—and I suspect many of my readers will be similarly deprived. But that doesn't mean we cannot appreciate their qualities (and their occasional shortcomings) with a detachment which many owners may lack. And where it hasn't been possible to try out a particular model or

Symbols galore: the Ferrari badge linked with the Pininfarina emblem (a rare occurence) above the title of the super-exotic, super-rare, Superfast 500, perhaps Ferrari's most glamourous four seater

Without whom there would be no four seater Ferraris as we know them today

variant at first-hand, then I have unashamedly drawn upon the reactions and comments of more fortunate fellow journalists to help put a particular design in perspective.

Finally, a word on the actual subject of the book. Four-seat Ferraris imply almost a contradiction in terms, a sleek businessman's express rather than an out-and-out sports or GT car, an unworthy dilution of the original inspiration which made the name so universally respected. I can sympathize with the sentiment, but as an engineer, I don't agree with it. To my mind, the four-seat Ferraris have included some of the most interesting and ambitious of the company's production-car designs, and the way in which they have managed to combine performance and practicality makes them greater design successes than some of their outwardly more glamorous two-seat stablemates. Read on, and see if you find yourself agreeing with me. . . .

Paris Show, 1956. Pinin Farina (left) father of Sergio Pininfarina (right); Ferrari body designers by appointment

Chapter 1
The parentage

The story of the four-seat Ferraris goes further back into the company's past than many of today's enthusiasts may realize; to the very beginning of its serious involvement with road-going production cars. Even today, most people probably still associate the company's name with the racing circuit rather than the showroom, an order of priorities which closely follows that of Enzo Ferrari himself. The first Ferraris were all specialized competition cars, and if owners were crazy enough to demand changes and modifications which turned a superb track machine into a wild and almost undrivable road projectile, then that was their own decision. All too often the result was a combination of phenomenal performance with razor-edge handling which demanded the reflexes of a top-class racing driver to keep under control, all delivered in a package with the comfort and elegance of a fighter cockpit. Whichever way you look at it, the result was a blend of virtues and vices which appealed to a fortunate few.

But over the years even the *Commendatore* woke up to the need for some compromises with his pure racing ideal. If there were some customers who were eccentric enough to want to use the blend of speed and roadholding which his cars provided, on the road rather than on the racetrack, and if they had the plentiful amounts of money needed to turn this wish into reality, then why shouldn't Ferrari

One of the earliest of the four-seaters—a one-off Superleggera show car by Touring on the 166S Ferrari at the Turin Salon of 1949

accommodate them? The money they paid in such quantity all helped to pay the ever-increasing racing bills, and slowly but inevitably, the company began to include occasional orders for fast but comparatively comfortable road cars, in among the racing machinery. They were individual, made in small numbers, and no two were totally identical.

Yet production cars remained very much part of the background until the middle 1950s. It was only in 1951 that Ferrari seemed to change his mind, though in truth it was anything but change for change's sake. Like many other racing fanatics before and since, he was finding that costs were rising out of control, and if he was to retain that independence from outside sponsorship on which he insisted, then some other way had to be found of earning the money to pay the bills. Since there seemed to be a steady market for road-going Ferraris, why not make a profit by feeding that market on a properly efficient, series-production basis? This would use as much in the way of ideas,

designs and materials as possible from the racing department, and involve almost no diversion of effort from Ferrari's primary purpose, the building of racing cars which could beat the world's opposition.

Up to then, Ferrari had simply built the engines, chassis and mechanical parts, handing the skeletons over to whichever of Italy's top coachbuilders the individual buyer had chosen to clothe his car. Now he needed to build up a close business relationship with a designer and body builder who could become a partner in this new part of his empire. For such an independently minded autocrat, this was a difficult step, as Griff Borgeson described in *Ferrari, the Man, the Machines*, 'Enzo must have seen it all coming in 1951, when he opened negotiations with Pininfarina, who was still rather a small operator but whose outstanding talent Ferrari obviously recognized. Pinin describes this bourgeois courtship most entertainingly. Ferrari sent word to Turin through an emissary that

Right *The sleek fastback of Touring's coupés on the 166, 195 and 212 Ferraris looked stylish but left meagre headroom for rear-seat passengers*

Far right *First of a long line of varied and ingenious body designs from Ferrari's most successful collaborator: Pininfarina's 212 coupé*

he would like to have a word with Pinin in far-off Modena. Pinin's response to the command performance was to tell the intermediary that he would be happy to meet with Signor Ferrari . . . in Turin. This game seemed to go on interminably, with the two men avoiding each other, Pinin says, like two fish in a bowl. Neither would give in. Finally, "a Solomonic solution was found: we would meet on neutral ground, in Tortona".

'Pinin won this round, with Ferrari having to travel the longer distance by far. But he did not win the next one, when he tried to persuade Ferrari to come and see his very fine factory. Ferrari made it clear that he went nowhere to see anyone, period, end of discussion. Pinin accepted Ferrari's character as he found it, and the courtship was concluded successfully . . . to the astonishment of all, it turned out to be a marriage made in heaven, each obstinate man having total confidence in, and respect for, the other. They complemented each other, Pinin says, "like a pair of clasped hands".

'The wedding resulted in the creation of Ferrari's GT car division, committed to the production of no

COUPÉ 2 POSTI + 2 DI FORTUNA SU FERRARI 212 INTER

Pinin Farina

TORINO · CORSO TRAPANI 107-115
INDIRIZZO TELEGRAFICO: "PININCAR"

more than a thousand cars per year [ambitious, to say the least], Pininfarina becoming an effective partner in the affair. Thus Ferrari was able to finance the one thing in life which he claimed to care anything about'.

All the same, actually designing and building the first prototypes of this initial production series took the best part of three years. The engine, as usual with Ferrari, was no problem at all: the various competition cars had produced a legacy of different sizes and parts which could be reassembled to produce a power unit of almost any size and characteristics needed. From the original postwar Ferrari Grand Prix cars, Ferrari engines had been almost entirely 60 degree V12s, with slightly over-square bore/stroke ratios in the interests of greater piston area and lower piston speed and acceleration. The original supercharged 1.5 litre Formula One engine had been designed by Colombo, who left Ferrari in 1949, but before his departure he had sketched the outline of an unblown engine, the 166, which was finished by Aurelio Lampredi and used in the first sports-racing Ferrari. This engine, in its original form, had 60 mm cylinder bores and a 58.8 mm stroke, producing a capacity of 1995 cc. With a single overhead camshaft for each cylinder bank, and a double-choke Weber carburettor, it produced 150 bhp on 8.5:1 compression, and proved highly successful, in its own right and as the basis for a whole family of developments. (Already I am in trouble with power outputs. Several sources quote 150 bhp for the 166, others say no more than 110!)

But Lampredi had ideas of his own on engine design. Setting weight and simplicity at least as high as Colombo's ideals of large piston area and low stresses on his list of priorities, he was to bring Ferrari what he most wanted—the Grand Prix World Championship—by abandoning the super-charged option and aiming instead at the 4.5 litre capacity limit then allowed by the rules for unblown engines. This he did in stages. He took the *tipo* 166 engine which was already doing well in Formula Two, and opened the bores out to 68 mm, increasing the capacity to 2563 cc and the power to 200 bhp when racing. Then a second stage followed from that new *tipo* 212 in the shape of the (early) 275 engine, which had the bore widened to 72 mm and the stroke lengthened to 68 mm, raising the capacity to 3322 cc and the power to 300 bhp. This last engine was for sports-racing only. Finally, the process was completed (after an interim 80 by 68 mm, 4102 cc, 335 bhp *tipo* 340 engine) by the Championship-winning *tipo* 375, with 80 mm bore, 74.5 mm stroke, 4494 cc, and 350 bhp. All these engines had the same V12 configuration with a single overhead camshaft per cylinder bank, and the different measurements would show up again and again in the Ferrari story. By 1952 for example, the 68 mm bores of the 212 engine had been matched with the 68 mm stroke of the 340 to produce one of the few square engines Ferrari has ever built. The total capacity was 2963 cc, and with nine to one compression and a trio of double-choke Webers suitable for racing it turned out 240 bhp at 7200 rpm. This was the *tipo* 250 and it powered the car which was entered by Giovanni Bracco in the 1952 Mille Miglia—the 250 Sport coupé. It was scarcely a promising entry, as the hard-drinking, chain-smoking Bracco (who was to earn a unique place in the record books as the winner of every one of the six Biella to Oropa hillclimbs held between 1939 and 1956) had too few tyres to stand a reasonable chance of finishing, let alone against the all-conquering Mercedes-Benz works team which was chalking up victories in most of the classic sports-car races of Europe.

But the car proved both fast and supremely reliable. Unfortunately, by the time he entered Pescara, the canvas was showing through on his

Another variation on the 212 Inter—this time by Ghia. The car was described as a berlina (saloon)—the next time the word was used officially for a Ferrari was to be the Pinin of 30 years later

last set of tyres, and Bracco was only able to continue at all by fitting a stopgap set which were actually too small for the car. Then, as they plunged down the hairpin descent of the Futa Pass, the weather turned wet, and the balance tilted towards

16

the Italian driver. The damp conditions slowed down both the tyre wear, and the Mercedes. Bracco pulled into the lead, and stayed there to the finish. Ferrari was delighted with the result, and the car was renamed the 250MM in honour of the victory.

Mid-Fifties Ferrari: the elegant and remarkably undated 250GT Europa had a three litre engine. Fitted with a bigger 4.5 litre unit in the same chassis it became the 375 America for the Transatlantic trade

By 1953, Ferrari was turning out a mixed bag of production GT cars, including the 375 America, which despite the similarity in designation to the interim 375 Formula One car, had an entirely revized engine, and the 250 Europa, which was essentially the same car fitted with a smaller three-litre unit better suited to European conditions. The 375 had wider bores at 84 mm rather than the 80 mm of the 375F1, balanced by a shorter stroke of 64 mm rather than the 74.5 mm of the original—the resulting capacity was very slightly larger at 4523 cc rather than 4494, and power in road trim was 300 bhp at 6000 rpm. The 250 Europa, on the other hand, used the square 68 mm by 68 mm Mille Miglia engine, with slightly lower compression, detuned to 200 bhp rather than the 240 of the original.

What Ferrari now had in mind was to replace both these versions with an entirely new GT car, a single design which would form the basis of a much higher production output, and which would fulfil the needs of as many customers as possible. One of the problems with the Europa had been the heavy handling, so the new car was given a shorter and more compact chassis, with a wheelbase 20 cm less than the Europa. Pininfarina's body shape for the car was almost identical to the design he produced for both the Europa and the America, the slight reduction in overall length made the car look more purposeful and better balanced. Nor was this an illusion: the traditional independent front suspension set up of a transverse leaf spring was replaced by a much more precise and efficient arrangement of unequal upper and lower wishbones and coil springs. The rear suspension came in for less drastic treatment—the live axle was carried on a pair of semi-elliptic springs and located by parallel trailing arms, but this time the main chassis members passed above rather than underneath the axle. But the shorter chassis was only made possible by the most radical change between this 250 and the version which preceded it: the replacement of the square 68 by 68 mm engine by an entirely new engine of similar capacity. New, that is, for a road Ferrari, as the engine involved had already appeared on a racing machine, ironically at the same time as the Mille Miglia appearance of the square three litre it was now ousting on the production line. This engine was in fact yet another derivation of the original Colombo design, with the 58.8 mm stroke first seen on the 166 Sports, Formula 2 and Mille Miglia designs of 1948, but now matched with a wider 73 mm bore, producing a capacity of 2953 cc. In 1952 racing trim, the engine had delivered 230 bhp, and this was enough to provide some encouraging results, amid some real disappointments. In the 1953 Mille Miglia, Hawthorn's car had had to retire with brake trouble, while Marzotto's caught fire. Others suffered persistent problems with rear axle breakages, and although the car did better in American racing, it was left behind in the sporting

By Boano's standards a sober and understated design: a classic 250GT treatment with only rudimentary tailfins, and the family pedigree showing through very clearly

arena by Ferrari turning to larger and more powerful sports cars.

Yet this same engine was to provide the motive power for what would become the most successful production Ferrari by far. Fitted with a trio of double-choke Webers (rather than the four-choke carbs of the competition car), the engine pushed out a useful 220 bhp. Linked to a four-speed all-synchro gearbox and a twin dry-plate clutch, it provided tractable power in plenty for a car which, by the standards of its time, set new levels of response and handling.

Not surprisingly, the car sold well from the beginning. The new 250GT, still called—confusingly—the Europa, made its debut at the Paris Motor Show in October 1954, with car no. 0357GT. The initial production series of these cars made the confusion worse by using sheet steel panelled bodies made originally by Pininfarina for the earlier Europa, and though a definite style was set from the start, there were still detail differences in areas like door pillars and window lines. Ten of the three dozen cars which made up the original production batch through to the Brussels Show of January 1956 had non-standard bodies, but even so only one of these, a design by Michelotti for Princess de Rethy of the Belgian royal family, was not by Ferrari's chief collaborator, Pininfarina.

As time went by, other coachbuilders were able to try their hands at making bodies for the 250GT, including Boano of Turin, and their successors Ellena. In most cases, they were executing Pininfarina's designs, sometimes with additions, embellishments and detail treatments of their own, although occasionally they were able to build the prototype for a new model in the range. For as the success of the 250GT continued, more and more versions came to be offered: spiders and cabriolets and an ever-widening choice of coupés and berlinette. But as the Fifties came to an end, a vital gap in the model range was beginning to become more and more apparent.

The 250GT had transformed Ferrari's status from a highly talented but small-scale producer of racing machinery into a genuine car maker in his own right. In the five years leading up to the model's introduction, Ferrari had turned out almost two hundred road cars altogether, some even with an attempt at four seats. By the time the 250 range was replaced a decade later, the company was turning out more than six hundred production cars in a single year, a sixteenfold increase which was to provide the finance for ever more ambitious racing efforts. But the competition, from rivals like Maserati and Aston Martin, was becoming keener, and they were able to offer the buyer something which Ferrari, for all his success, could not.

Chapter 2
The first of the breed

So far, all the production Ferraris made, whatever the size of their engines or the style of their bodywork, had one important feature in common. They were intended for a driver and just one passenger, at least so far as any real space was concerned. Most of them only had two seats anyway. Those which offered more accommodation were few in number and grudging in the space they provided: occasional seats which really lived up to their name were shoe-horned into a chassis made for a two-seater, and anyone forced to spend any time in them would opt for train travel, or staying at home, next time the opportunity arose.

To be fair to Ferrari, there were sound reasons for this policy. More than any other maker in the world, his road cars were based on his racing designs, and since none of these ever had more than two seats anyway, producing a viable four-seater made a much more radical re-design necessary. Already the 250GT had shown how the handling of the old Europa could be transformed by shortening the chassis. But this meant the design was more restricted than before in its interior space, and there was less chance than ever of finding space for another pair of occupants. In the old days, the conclusion would have been simple, and inescapable: if you wanted four seats, you bought two Ferraris, or you saved your money by buying some lesser vehicle.

There was one argument, and only one, which could alter this. By the late Fifties, Ferrari's increasing domination of the super-GT market was being challenged by other illustrious names, among them Aston Martin, whose beautiful DB4 had shown that it was possible to provide style, performance and four seats in the same civilized and desirable package. Older rivals Maserati were weighing in with the 3500GT which, though still no more a four-seater than some of the earlier attempts by Ferrari buyers to have their automotive cake and eat it, still had potential in this direction with generous luggage room behind the front seats which could conceivably be put to other uses.

The shape of things to come: the bigger, but still beautifully balanced proportions of Pininfarina's prototype on the longer chassis, a worthy competitor for the DB4 Aston Martin

So Ferrari, and Pininfarina, set to work to produce a genuine four-seat version of the 250GT. Stretching the chassis was out: they had somehow to find the extra space they needed within the already proven package of the existing frame. So the wheelbase remained the same, at 260 cm (though a shorter 240 cm version was on the way for the Berlinetta SWB and the Spider California) but the front and rear track measurements were widened by four centimetres or so apiece. The only way to open out the interior was to move the engine forward in the frame by a total of eight inches, or twenty centimetres—by now the power unit was to be the version used in the latest 250GT cabriolets, which used coil valve springs and had the inlet manifolds in the Vee with the exhausts, and the sparking plugs on the outside of the cylinder banks. The 240 bhp engine was harnessed to a four-speed gearbox with electrically operated British built Laycock de Normanville overdrive.

Pininfarina's body design was a real *tour de force*. In spite of the need to provide room for twice as many occupants, the shape still managed to retain the compactness of a coupé rather than the portliness of a saloon. Although the chassis was substantially the same size as before, there was more overhang, particularly at the rear, and the car was now a foot longer than its stable-mates. But careful wind-tunnel testing had helped produce a shape which was efficient aerodynamically and which, though clearly much more massive than the two-seater, was still clean and elegant and impressive. Meanwhile, the rear seats, which were after all the object of the whole exercise, were comfortable enough to make a journey of reasonable length possible. Though headroom was on the short side, because of the downsweep of the roofline, they were ideal for growing children or passengers of Italian rather than Scandinavian height.

The early production prototype of 1960, with reflectors mounted above the rear bumpers and louvres cut into the rear quarter pillars

Another view of the 250GTE 2+2 prototype shows off its broader beam, and the bodywork almost devoid of ornamentation, apart from the long horizontal crease along the sides

Next page *Why so many people still thought that REAL Ferraris should only have two seats—the classic, clean and compact shape of the Ferrari 250GT*

The initial pre-production prototype of the car carried chassis number 1287GT and had the basic body shape of the future production model, in this case panelled in silver with red leather interior, but there were some small detail differences. The generous side window area ended in a small rear-quarter panel opposite the bottom of the rear screen—what the Americans call a 'sail panel'—and on this car, the panel was pierced with a set of louvres for air extraction. The side panelling of the car was otherwise devoid of any holes, intakes or louvres or lights, save only a longitudinal line just above the top of the wheel arches to reduce the impact of such a large area of almost flat metalwork. The car was finished in the spring of 1959, and was then put through a detailed (and highly secret) test and development programme. By March of 1960, it was clear that Ferrari and Pininfarina had a

The magnificent Ferrari V12 engine, a masterpiece of the engineer's art—its ample reserves of power and reliability provided the driving force for the Commendatore's *increasingly successful four-seat models*

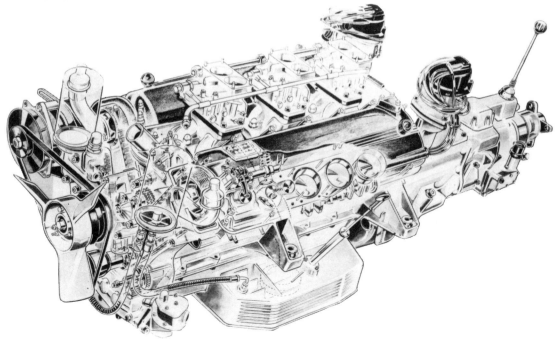

potential winner on their hands, and the project went through to the next stage of development.

By the end of that month of March, two more chassis—1895GT and 1903GT—were taking shape in the workshops at Modena, and Pininfarina was assembling bodies to be fitted to them. The first to be completed was 1895GT, which had a body painted in brilliant Italian racing red with brown leather upholstery. As on the original car, the headlights were mounted in chrome surrounds in the front

Backing into the limelight: Ferrari's first 2+2 makes its initial public appearance in the discreet seclusion of the Le Mans 24 Hour Race—the flag on the front identifies it as the course marshal's car

By the Paris Show of 1960 the car had been given another set of louvres on the frong wing rather than on the rear quarter

wings, with a pair of fog lights set at either end of the small radiator grille, just above the chrome front bumper bar. By now, legal requirements in Italy specified the fitting of repeater lights for the direction indicators on the sides of the front wings, but these were still, apart from the horizontal line, the only embellishments on the smooth side surfaces of the car. Even the louvres from the rear quarters had been removed on this car.

Normally, any car as new and as commercially important as this would be shown off to the public on a stand at one of the classic international motor shows, but in this case Ferrari had something else in mind. The car was completed by the middle of June, just before the running of the Le Mans 24-Hour race, at which the Ferrari team colours would be carried by three-litre prototypes which had a similar pedigree to the new car. So Ferrari handed the precious new prototype over to the course marshals to use as official transport for the duration of the meeting.

As a public relations gesture, it was superb. Not only did it put the car on show before the sporting public at one of the biggest events on the competition calendar, it gave it the accolade of official patronage by the Le Mans organizers, the Automobile Club de l'Ouest. And to fill Ferrari's cup to overflowing, the race cars hammered the opposition, such as it was, into the concrete by taking all save one of the first seven places. The message was crystal clear: the new car might look heavier, bigger and more respectable than the 250GT Ferraris, but

The original 250GTE 2+2 was big and rather portly by Ferrari standards—but the clean simple body shape carried few styling embellishments

The 250GTE 2+2 was the nearest Ferrari had yet approached to genuine series production, but even then there were detail differences between individual cars. This early production version has auxiliary lamps set into the radiator grille, louvres in a wing panel and broad chrome headlamp surrounds but no side marker lights

its chassis and power plant still had a great deal in common with the cars which had just won one of the world's toughest races. The 250GTE 2+2 was clearly every inch a Ferrari.

The body of the second prototype was finished at the same time as the first one was completed. The car itself was painted white, with red leather upholstery; it was used for advertising and publicity photographs for the new model. Not until the fourth

car—confusingly, this was identified as the third prototype and the first actual production car—was the 250GTE 2+2 actually put on show. This was chassis no. 2031GT, and it was earmarked for the Turin Show at the end of October: but it was beaten to the stands by three later cars in that initial production batch. Two were shown at Paris early in October, chassis nos. 2043GT and 2169GT. Another—the first right-hand-drive version of the

This pre-production prototype, featured in the original sales brochure of 1960 had wing louvres and auxiliary lamps, with repeater lights mounted low down in front of the wheelarches

*The 1961–62 production
version of the 250GTE 2+2
had the side repeater lights
streamlined and mounted
higher up on the horizontal
panel line—and the wing
louvres were cut into a
separate panel fitted into the
wing rather than into the
wing panel itself*

car, chassis no. 2185GT—was shown at Earls Court in the middle of the month.

Even now, detail differences were persisting between one car and another. The production versions had louvres in the front wings between the wheel arch and the door opening—on some cars the louvres were cut directly into the body panelling, while on others they were cut into a rectangular panel which was itself fitted into the wing panel. The radiator-mounted foglamps vanished on the first production cars too.

Comfort and visibility inside the car were good. The driver and front passenger each had individual bucket seats with reclining backs, and the small rear seat was divided by a central armrest, while the generous window area gave everyone a good view. Speedometer, rev-counter and oil-pressure gauge sat in a binnacle behind the steering wheel, with the other instruments mounted in a central dashboard. The front and rear quarter-lights on each side

Another view of the 1961–62 version shows the auxiliary lamps at the ends of the radiator grille

1963—and the car is substantially unchanged. The wing louvre panel remains (though hard to spot in this picture) and the auxiliary lamps have moved to a new position beneath the headlamps

Very few changes from the original design: the central bonnet ridge stops at the front of the panel rather than continuing to the Ferrari badge, but otherwise the body is still remarkably similar to that of the first prototype

opened, and the door windows could be fitted with electric winders as extra options.

But with a car like this, everything depended on how it performed on the road. Careful wind-tunnel testing helped allow a useful 150 mph top speed, and although the bigger body imposed a slight weight penalty, this was small enough to allow a respectable response to the throttle pedal, particularly for a potential four-seater. The handling was rather more difficult to assess. The chassis was already well proven, but shifting the engine further forward did alter the weight distribution and increase the understeering tendency. But that could be coped with, as Alain Bertaut found when testing the car for the French magazine *Moteurs* at Montlhéry in 1961 '. . . and so to take the curves quickly required an abrupt movement of the steering wheel, breaking the rear wheels loose into a lateral slide, and then controlling the slippage with the accelerator and the steering wheel'. Not quite the technique for a busy morning on the Kingston Bypass perhaps, but the kind of handling on which most Ferraris thrive, and it allowed Bertaut to record his fastest lap on the circuit with any GT car.

Though many enthusiasts remained rather dubious about the whole idea of a family four-seater Ferrari, and the model has consistently rated relatively low on the latter-day collectors' market, it was a commercial success from the very beginning. With detail alterations, like the fitting of foglamps outside the radiator grille, and changes in the shape of the rear-light assemblies, wider wheels and larger valves for the engine, a second series of 356 cars succeeded the initial 299-car run in 1962, and this was followed in turn by another 300 car series for 1963. By the time the last of the cars, chassis number 4961GT, emerged from the shops, almost a thousand had been made. Four-seat Ferraris were obviously here to stay.

Chapter 3
Bigger and better?

By the time the 250GTE 2+2 had come to the end of its three-year production run, it was still very much the same car which had made such a dramatic appearance at Le Mans in 1960. There had been progressive changes and improvements: larger valves, lighter pistons and connecting rods for the engine, coil springs to back up the rear hydraulic shock-absorbers, a separate oil supply for the gearbox and the overdrive unit, larger stabilizer bars for the front suspension, and so on. But by 1963, the performance race was beginning to leave the 250GT 2+2 behind, and it seemed to Ferrari that something bigger and more powerful was needed to maintain the momentum in the market place.

Already plans were afoot which would result in the 250GTE's successor making its appearance, with a larger engine, at the beginning of 1964. But as a stopgap, the last 50 bodies made at Pininfarina's workshops for the 2+2 were fitted with the first of the larger engines. The power unit itself was another incarnation of the original Colombo V12, but its measurements were linked to another pile of parts bins in the Modena workshops, belonging to a different design altogether.

In 1955, financial crises forced the Lancia company to back out of the ruinously expensive world of Grand Prix racing. They handed over all their cars, engines, machinery and personnel to Ferrari. Part of the package was the talented Vittorio Jano, who

Built in late 1963, this example has the one-piece tail-lights and the front-end treatment of a late-production 250GTE 2+2. If it also had an 'America' tag on the bootlid, it would be one of the rare hybrids which were fitted with the four-litre engine developed for the car's 330GT successor

This one also looks like a 250GTE—but it is in fact a pre-production 330GT, lacking details like the revized rear-end shape and the altered side-window contour

had worked with Ferrari before the war when they had jointly master-minded Alfa Romeo's racing organization. Jano was one of those brilliant individuals who tended never to take anyone else's ideas for granted as solutions to engineering problems, preferring instead to explore unorthodox answers for himself. It so happened that Ferrari's only son, christened Alfredo but known to his father as Dino, had suggested the idea of a V6 engine not long before his tragically early death, from leukaemia, in 1956 at the age of only 24. Jano was a firm believer in the virtues of this configuration for engines with far fewer than 12 cylinders (where the Vee had always been compulsory to avoid the engine being ridiculously long) on the grounds of strength and balance. He had already designed

But the most obvious differences between the 330GT and its predecessors were apparent from the front: the wider grille and the quadruple headlamps

Next page *Four-seat Ferrari show car: late-version 250GTE or four-litre America? Only a look at the bootlid would tell for sure . . .*

successful engines for Lancia with the cylinder banks set at 60 degrees, and he now set about doing a similar job for Ferrari.

This engine, called after its original protagonist the Dino V6, was to be highly successful, powering Mike Hawthorn to his World Championship in 1958 in its 2.4 litre Formula One version. But it was unusual, in that Jano widened the angle between the cylinder banks from the theoretically ideal 60 degrees to 65 degrees. He had a sound reason for this: with a 60 degree Vee, there simply wasn't enough room for the inlet tracts to have the gentle curves which would allow efficient induction. Changing the angle was supposed to cause all kinds of problems with out-of-balance forces—but Jano solved them by effectively treating each pair of cylinders separately for timing purposes. Some crankpins were spaced at 55 degrees (which, with the 65 degrees between the banks, produced the ideal 120 degree spacing between explosions), and others were spaced at 185 degrees—120 degrees plus the 65 degree vee angle. The net result of these arrangements was six evenly spaced explosions for two complete engine revolutions, each 120 degrees apart.

No such contrivances were necessary for the classic V12 however. But the bigger engine used in the 250GTE's successor did use two parameters of the earlier engine. In its original Formula Two version of 1956, the Dino engine had 70 mm bores with a stroke of 64.5 mm, producing a total capacity of 1489 cc and an output of 180 bhp in racing trim. By 1957, an interim Formula One version had been produced—as with Lampredi's engines of the late 40s, the increase in size from 1.5 to 2.5 litres was carried out in stages—called the Dino 196/F1 which had a swept volume of 1983 cc. This was achieved by widening the bores to 77 mm and lengthening the stroke to 71 mm. Although the F1 engine was soon

Two views (left) that show the external differences between the 250GTE and the 330GT. The side window line ends in a sharper corner at the rear end, the tail of the car has more pronounced flanks, with the rear lamps mounted in horizontal clusters (top) while the wing louvres are cut in an irregular row and the roofline follows a more streamlined curve (bottom)

The production 330GT (next page) was a handsome car, but its size and styling details met with a lot of criticism from Ferrari fans at the time

43

MODENA **Ferrari** ITALIA

PRESENTA LA NUOVA FERRARI 330 GRAN TURISMO

La vettura costruita
in piccola serie che compendia l'esperienza
delle corse

ECCO UN ALTRO GIOIELLO DEL CAVALLINO RAMPANTE

Carrozzata da *pininfarina*
3.967 cc. - 12 cilindri - 300 CV

La Shell è lieta di avere sempre
unito il suo nome alla **Ferrari**
in tutte le competizioni tecnico-sportive
in tutti i primati raggiunti, in
tutte le vittorie conquistate dal
"cavallino rampante"

SUPERSHELL CON ICA —— SHELL X 100 MOTOR OIL
sono il contributo della Shell
alle affermazioni della **Ferrari**

widened out to 85 mm to produce Hawthorn's title-winning Dino 246 version, the 77 by 71 mm configuration was used (with a 60 degree vee and revised crankpin spacing) in the 196 Sports and GT six-cylinder two-litre units.

But a bore and a stroke which added up to almost two litres in a V6 would be nicely suited to an almost four-litre version of the classic V12, and so it proved. The 77 mm bore, 71 mm stroke prescription appeared in twelve-cylinder form in 1960, in the 340 bhp, 3967 cc 400/SA unit used to power the 400 Superamerica. And three years later it appeared again, with identical dimensions and 8.8:1 compression, with a slightly less ambitious power peak of 290 bhp, as the 330/GT unit, intended for the 250GTE's replacement.

This was the engine which was fitted into the last 50 of those 250GTE 2+2s. Clearly there had to be some distinction made between these four-litre cars and the three-litre version which carried the same bodywork. The hybrids were called the 330 America, and some (though apparently not all) actually carried an 'America' label on the bodywork. The chassis numbers began with 4953GT and ended at 5125GT. Outwardly, there was no other difference at all from the three-litre cars, which did in fact conceal some quite important changes to the engines used.

The idea of fitting a four-litre engine into the three-litre car went right back to the very beginning of the model run, when the four-litre Superamerica 400 was being produced alongside it at Modena. A special one-off car, numbered in the Superamerica series (2257SA) was built for Enzo Ferrari himself, and was nothing less than a 250GTE 2+2 with the Superamerica engine. At the time, no other cars of this type were built, but it did at least prove that the exercise was feasible. When it was repeated on a series basis three years later though, there were

The kind of background in which the 330GT was meant to feel at home

Left *Threefold partnership: Shell, Pininfarina and Ferrari collaborate on this advertisement to introduce the 330GT, and to remind their customers that even big and luxurious models like this have the family competition pedigree under the skin*

Next page *By 1965 the factory had decided the four headlamp layout was a mixed blessing—later cars switched back to just two headlights*

Other detail changes are more apparent in this view (above) *including restyled wing vents, wraparound sidelights, and the moving of the Pininfarina badge from the front wing to the rear*

problems which arose from improvements made to the engine in the meantime. To improve the circulation of the cooling water between the widened cylinders, the bore centres were set 94 mm apart instead of 90 mm apart, in a revized block. This also made it possible to reposition the sparking plugs for more efficient combustion, but it made the engine appreciably longer, which did result in clearance problems in the 330 America.

These were taken care of in its successor, the 330GT 2+2 proper, as this was a substantially new car altogether. The chassis was still assembled from electrically-welded steel tubes of oval section, two large tubes forming the main fore-and-aft members with various cross-connections to produce a light but rigid frame for the car. But the wheelbase was a fraction longer than its predecessor, at 265 cm, and while the rear track was 5 mm narrower at 1389 mm, the front track was widened by no less than 43 mm to 1397 mm. To make the very most of these modest changes, the new Pininfarina body was altogether larger and roomier than the earlier design. There was more room for the rear-seat passengers, thanks to the longer body, and the reshaped contours which added to the back-seat headroom. There was more room for four people's luggage, thanks to the larger and more rounded tail end to the car, and although the overall dimensions were very much the same, the result was a car which looked much larger and heavier all round. It still bore more than just a passing family resemblance to the car it replaced, but there were some changes with which many Ferrari-fanciers were less than happy. The wing-mounted louvres were respaced in three groups of three rather than in a single row, the longitudinal crease along the side panels was far less obvious, the radiator grille was made both shallower and considerably wider and, most obviously of all, each of the two headlamps had a smaller long-range lamp mounted inboard in a chromed elliptical enclosure. There were other alterations under the skin, too: the gearbox and transmission were strengthened to cope with the extra horsepower delivered by the new engine, the rear dampers were replaced by adjustable Konis, and the front and rear brakes were divided into two separate systems.

Even portly and luxurious four-seaters like the 330GT manage to be competition contenders under the skin— like this British-registered example of 1964 leaning into a bend in a club race

Many enthusiasts—and motoring journalists— criticized the car because it looked too large, and too flabby, for a real Ferrari. Those who looked at the design on its own merits, rather than by simply comparing it with what had gone before, were less sure. And those who were fortunate enough to look at the car as a means of family transport with the excitement and performance of a real Ferrari, soon realized that its performance belied any impression of a simple luxury express which its well-rounded lines might suggest. They voted, in very large numbers, with their cheque books.

Once again, in producing a four-seater road car, Ferrari had succeeded in confounding all his critics and getting it right, in marketing terms. The 330GT

Next page The standard production 330GT of 1966: though wire wheels were available to order, the standard version had these alloy disc wheels with knock-off hubs

2+2 went on to break the records set up by its 250GT predecessor, and during the model's four-year production run, a total of around 100 cars had been built and sold. In the summer of 1965, a redesigned second-series version of the 330GT 2+2 was introduced, which did go some way towards meeting earlier criticisms of the styling. The controversial four-headlamp set up was replaced by a single lamp in each front wing, the side louvres were redesigned and the Borrani wire wheels were replaced by Campagnolo alloy wheels as standard fittings.

Other changes included the replacement of the four-speed box and overdrive by a conventional five-speed transmission. The four-point mounting by which the engine was carried on the chassis frame was changed to a two-point mounting to cut down the transmission of noise and vibration from the power unit to the body, and the clutch, brake and accelerator pedals were changed from the organ-pedal type to the pendant type, suspended from above. These last two changes were introduced in 1966, after the introduction of the 330GTC with its five-speed transaxle at Geneva, which had the same features. Electric cooling fans became obvious about this time too although they may have come earlier. Other options, intended to add to the luxury of the car, were available to special order—air conditioning and power steering, which added up to two more steps away from the Spartan appointments of traditional Ferraris.

In all, 625 first-series cars were made in a year and a half, together with another 455 of the series II versions, making a grand total of 1080, a highly respectable figure for a producer like Ferrari. But the 330GT 2+2, successful as it was, wasn't the only four-seat Ferrari made during the middle Sixties—set alongside it was a larger, and much rarer, model altogether.

Chapter 4
Super fast-super rare

Side by side with the long list of production cars built mainly for the European market, ran another theme in Ferrari's thinking: larger, more powerful models which were intended to give him a larger share of the all-important American trade. During the early Fifties, when the blown Colombo-designed racing V12 of 1.5 litres was being stretched through a succession of larger versions by Aurelio Lampredi to produce the final unblown 4.5 litre Grand Prix engine, several of these power units were tried out in sports cars too. Because of the considerably wider cylinder bores needed to treble the engine's capacity, Lampredi shifted the cylinder bores further apart—from 90 mm between centres up to 108 mm, which produced a much longer engine than the original Colombo V12. Since sealing between block and heads also proved a problem with the high compression ratios used in racing, Lampredi fitted fixed cylinder heads which had the cylinder liners screwed into them to provide a gas tight joint.

The interim 4.1 litre version of this engine made its racing appearance in the Swiss Grand Prix in the summer of 1950, and by the Paris Show of the following October a sports car was exhibited with a detuned 220 bhp version of the 80 by 68 mm 340 series engine. By the Turin Show of March 1951, Carrozzeria Touring were able to show a coupé they had built on the engine and chassis of this sports car, which became the 340 America. Its chassis number was 0122A, and following close behind it from the shops was 0130AL, this time bodied by Ghia as one of the earliest Ferrari 2+2s. But these were early days: of the 22 cars built, only eight were road cars rather than track cars, and these differed very much from one another, being mainly two-seaters. Only at the end of 1952 did Ferrari make a more positive effort to turn the America into a road car. The new model, the 342 America, retained the 4.1 litre Lampredi engine, but with a new all-synchro four-speed gearbox in place of the racing five-speed box of the original, a stronger transmission and a wider-track chassis.

The 342 America set the style for the series of models which followed it. With 200 bhp on tap from just over four litres, flexibility was good, stress levels low, and bodybuilders were able to indulge themselves in elaborate and luxurious designs. But this was before the days of series production, and only half a dozen cars were built, three coupés and two cabriolets by Pininfarina and another cabriolet by Vignale. In 1953, when the 250 Europa was in

First stage in the Superfast story: the Pininfarina-designed Superfast II prototype first appeared at the Turin Show of 1960

production, its place in the larger-model line was taken by the 375 America, which used the same chassis and body, but powered by a wider-bore, shorter-stroke 84 by 64 mm version of the V12 which had a capacity of 4523 cc and 50 per cent more power than its predecessor. Once again production was small: only a dozen or so cars were made in a variety of styles.

By the time the 250GT in its various versions had begun to dominate Ferrari's hopes for the European market, the 375 America was to give way to the first

By 1963 the body shape of this Coupé Aerodynamico, *based on the longer wheelbase version of the Superamerica had become sleeker*

Next page *At last, the 500 Superfast—the steadily evolving bodystyle which began with the Superfast prototypes—goes into production in this elegant, exotic and extremely rare four-seater*

Pininfarina's design for the 500 Superfast was a real tour de force: *somehow the car looked leaner, lighter and smaller than it really was*

of a new series, the 410 Superamerica, which appeared in chassis form at the Paris Show of 1955. The first series of fifteen cars was built on a longer 280 cm chassis—the engine used the 68 mm stroke of the original 340 America, but with a completely new set of 88 mm bores to provide a capacity of 4962 cc, turning out a lazy 340 bhp at 6000 rpm. It was a big, fast, long-legged car, as Dean Batchelor emphasized '. . . the Superamerica was built for cross-country touring and can cover long distances at high speeds with disconcerting ease. It is a car that is more at home in that environment than in the city or on winding mountain roads where maneuverability is of paramount importance'. Admittedly, its handling was on the heavy side, even compared with other

Ferraris, but all the same it stayed in production for three years, albeit in very small numbers.

The first series numbered 15 cars, one bodied by Ghia, two by Boano and the rest by Pininfarina. In 1958 another eight were built on the shorter 260 cm wheelbase chassis used for the three litre cars, and in 1959 an uprated version of the engine rated at 360 bhp was fitted with a wider track version of the 260 cm chassis and larger brake drums to produce the series III version, another 13 of which were built, all with Pininfarina bodies in different styles.

The final stage in the Superamerica story came in 1960, with the Superamerica 400—but this was a very different car from the earlier ones which bore the name, and really the first stage in a new story altogether. The larger and larger versions of the long-block Lampredi engine used up to the five-litre 410 were replaced by the shorter-block Colombo version of the V12—in this case the 77 by 71 mm, 3967 cc version as used in the 330GT three years later, but turning out 340 bhp in this case to cope with an essentially heavier car. The chassis was new too, with a shorter 241.3 cm wheelbase, and compared with its predecessor the new car was faster and more manoeuvrable. But despite their size, the cars were strictly two-seaters, and even when the first series of 25 cars was followed by a second 23 in 1962, which reverted to the 260 cm wheelbase chassis, the extra space was used to provide more luggage space rather than any extra seats.

This was to be the last of the Superamericas, but—although the class was to be carried on under a different name, it was one with close ties with the Superamerica series. In 1956, Pininfarina had built an extravagantly finned show car on the 410 Superamerica chassis, which was the star of the Paris Show with its sleek lines and two-tone bodywork; it had been named the 'Superfast'. At the

Next page The side view of the Superfast showed how closely Pininfarina's body style came to the classic aerofoil section (apart from the chopped off tail end) in the days when designers felt differently about high-speed lift . . .

61

Turin Show a year later, Pininfarina showed a tidied-up version of the car which had lost the fins, but kept the name. In fact the revisions in the body shape of the series III Superamerica 410 owed a lot to the ideas Pininfarina put into the Superfast prototypes. But the Superfast II, which appeared at the Turin Show of 1960, while it had a distinct family resemblance to the earlier cars, was in fact blazing an entirely new design trail.

The side view of the car resembled an aero-foil section of an aircraft wing, the result of exhaustive wind-tunnel testing at a time when high-speed lift was not seen as the problem it is today. The bonnet swept down to the 'leading edge' represented by the very shallow radiator grille and the bumper. At the rear, the fast-back roofline curved down to an equally sharply etched 'trailing edge', and the precise profiles were emphasized by a horizontal chrome strip running between them, along the sides of the car. Based on the Superamerica 400, the show car was a superbly balanced combination of gentle curves which was a masterpiece of the designer's art, and the theme was extended still further with Superfast III, which appeared at the 1962 Geneva Show, with larger windows and a thermostatically controlled radiator intake. The car was once again based on the Superamerica 400, and this chassis was also used for Superfast IV, which followed almost immediately afterwards.

After the appearance of Superfast IV, which was never actually exhibited at a Motor Show, the name wasn't to reappear for more than a year. When it did, at the Geneva Show of March 1964, it was on a new production car, though it was immediately recognizable as an only slightly altered version of Superfast III and IV, at least so far as body design was concerned. Gone was the extra crease in the side panelling which ran backwards from the top of the front wheel arch on the two prototypes, and

Exotic against any background (right). The subtle curves of the 500 Superfast contrast sharply with the harsh contours of modern industrial architecture

Above *A first series 330GT
2+2 is readily distinguished
by its four headlamps seen by
many as a curious departure*

Left *The Ferrari 250GTE
tends to be understated and
underpriced. Handsome
Pininfarina 2+2 coachwork
should make them more
desirable*

Above *This is the single
headlamp second series
330GT 2+2 equipped with the
soon to be familiar cast alloy
wheels. Its long wheel base
chassis is often confused with
. . .*

. . . right *the 330GTC which
Pininfarina describe on their
publicity material as* Coupé 2
posti. *This is not a 2+2*

Ferrari 365 *pininfarina* GT 2+2

Above left *Ferrari 500 Superfast was just that. Note long tapering tail and wide Borrani wire wheels*

Below left *The first of the modern line. This is the 365GT4 2+2 manufactured between 1972 and 1976. Note absence of front air dam*

Above *Every Ferrari factory-produced piece of literature has a number, this brochure's is 19/68 which at least dates the car*

Left *400GT with automatic transmission. This shot was used by the British importer for publicity purposes, hence the special 'registration' plate*

Top *Beautiful in white, this 400i awaits a final wash and polish after all pre-delivery tests have been completed at the factory*

Above *In contrast, the same white car alongside one in dark blue. Note the black rear panel on the white car*

gone, too, were the four headlamps which had appeared on Superfast IV in place of the faired-in single headlamps on Superfast III. Instead, the new Superfast had exposed single headlamps, and a new sharply cut-of-tail instead of the sharp trailing edge of the prototypes' aerofoil section. Otherwise, apart from the removal of a small vent behind the rear wheel arch, the body was still much the same as before—but under the beautiful skin of the Superfast, there had been several mechanical changes.

The chassis was substantially the same as the frame of 265 cm wheelbase built for the 330GT, but larger wheels were fitted than hitherto, and the track was a fraction of an inch wider at front and rear than the four-litre cars. The engine was also larger, an unusual hybrid with the cylinder spacing (at 108 mm between bore centres) of a Lampredi engine, but the detachable cylinder heads of the Colombo designs. The bore and stroke measurements were those of the old 410 Superamerica: 88 by

Classic prescription for driver comfort—always a Ferrari preoccupation (below): main instruments behind the wheel, the gearlever ready to hand and the magic of the prancing-horse badge

68 mm for a total capacity of 4962 cc and, with 9:1 compression, a power peak of 360 bhp or 400 bhp, depending on which set of figures you chose to believe.

Either way, this was a big, powerful, and very luxurious car, even by Ferrari standards. *Practical Classics* tested a carefully maintained example in 1980 and found it was 'certainly a car which cries out to be used. Sitting behind the polished woodrim wheel, the Ferrari doesn't feel too big (it's actually some 3 in. longer than an S type Jaguar saloon), nor as you move away does it feel in any way intimidating; its take-off from rest is smooth and easy to effect, and would do credit to any family saloon'.

More reassuring to Ferrari enthusiasts were the other qualities which came to light during the test. 'The clutch travel is quite long, however, and it needs to be used, when the gear-change becomes light and precise.... As the speed increases, you can hear something of the equally traditional "Ferrari thrash" of the valve gear through the bulkhead, but

One of the all-time design classics? How many other designs of the late 1960s would look as modern as the Superfast seen through today's eyes?

75

generally this is a very civilized and quiet car, as befits its luxury image. . . . The steering is not particularly light at lower speeds, but like almost everything else on the car, improves the faster you go—as with the ride, which has the usual knobbly Ferrari feel at low speed but smooths out beautifully higher up . . . you have that almost unique sense of control and feel of the road which virtually every Ferrari ever made has possessed . . . every tiny movement of the car and every reaction from the controls seems to give you an instant and accurate mental picture of the road surface, and what the car is doing in relation to it'.

Qualities like these, added to the kind of power which could produce a top speed comfortably in excess of 150 mph, found a ready market, even at a price which made many potential buyers' eyes water. But rumour has it that the production was limited deliberately, to use the body which Pinin-

Four genuine seats, or in this case proper luggage space, were positively a feature of the exotic 500 Superfast

farina had evolved through the range of Superfast show cars, and a chassis which was in production anyway for the 330GT, as a neat and economical way of making a limited-production prestige model and, at the same time, to use up the stock of large engines which was left over from the older Superamerica 410. True or not—and it doesn't explain the apparent modifying of the engines along the way—the Superfast was only made in limited numbers. The first production series added up to 25 vehicles, and the customers included both the Shah of Iran and comedian and car-fanatic Peter Sellers. In the closing months of 1965, production of a second series began, which embodied the changes built into the 330GT a few months before. This amounted to another dozen cars, one of which also found its way to the Shah. Of these cars—less than 40 in number—eight were right hand drive versions for the British market.

Because of the leisurely production rate—one or two cars a month during the run of the second series, which ended in August 1966 with a right-hand-drive car for Colonel Ronnie Hoare of Maranello Concessionaries, Ferrari's British distributor—there was time to build a certain amount of individuality into each one, though the basic shape and appointments were standard. Several owners were not particularly interested in four seats (why not use the Rolls for trips with the family?), and some cars were finished with the extra space behind the front seats used purely for luggage. But the car was based on the 330GT 2+2 chassis, which was a successful four-seater, and some of the Superfasts certainly qualified as among the rarest, fastest and most exotic four-seaters, anywhere in the world. In time, there would be other contenders for that distinction (notably from Lamborghini), but as we shall see, this was a market which Ferrari was determined not to give up easily.

Chapter 5
Two tons – and 150mph

The last Superfast of 37 cars was delivered to its fortunate owner in August 1966, and the last 330GT 2+2 of more than a thousand left the factory a year or so later. But there was no question of Ferrari not being ready with a follow-up car to keep the seemingly buoyant four-seater market sector well supplied. When his new four-seater emerged from the workshops and on to the company stand at the Paris Motor Show in October 1967, it proved to be the heaviest and most luxurious, but also the most sophisticated mechanically, of all Ferrari's two-plus-twos to date.

The car's designation was the 365GT 2+2 which, to the initiated, was a clear indication of its origins. During the 1966 racing season, the works had raced the 365P prototype, which had been powered by a 4390 cc version of the Colombo classic. This engine was virtually a wider-bore version of the 77 by 71 mm engine used in the 330GT (and in its racing version, in the 330P), with the cylinders widened to 81 mm apiece. On an 8.8:1 compression, the engine delivered a useful 320 bhp at peak, and a road version was used, in the 265 cm chassis of the 330GT 2+2 but fitted with a sleek two-seat spider body, to produce the limited-production 365 California cars of 1966 and 1967.

In the meantime, however, Ferrari's two-seat customers had been catered for by one of the most beautiful and most sporting production cars ever offered by the company—the ageless 275GTB berlinetta. This had appeared in 1964, and under the beautifully shaped Pininfarina bodywork it had an entirely new chassis which, though it was built up from welded oval-section steel-tubes as before, now followed the lead of the racing Ferraris in offering independent rear suspension for the first time on a production Ferrari. This was essentially similar to the already familiar independent front end system, with unequal length wishbones, coil springs and hydraulic dampers mounted concentrically with the springs. The chassis, with the 'short' 240 cm wheelbase, was also used for the elegant 275GTS open two-seater introduced at the Paris Show of October 1964 alongside the berlinetta. Both cars had the gearbox, a five-speed unit, mounted at the back end of the car—as had already been done on the circuit cars—to even the weight distribution.

Using this independent suspension system on a four-seat car posed certain problems though. It was difficult to find room for the transmission and the

By October 1967, either the four-seater body shape was becoming more familiar—or Pininfarina was becoming more adept at streamlining its generous proportions in his design for the 365GT 2+2

rear seats at the back of the car, and four-seaters are prone to wider load variations at the rear of the car than are two seat cars. The chassis used for the car was that already found on the 330GT 2+2, with its 265 cm wheelbase, though with widened front and rear track; the coil-spring and wishbones rear suspension was fitted with two important changes from the set up used on the 275GTB. First, the gearbox remained amidships, in unit with the engine and connected, through a rigid torque tube, to the rear differential. This whole unit was mounted on rubber pads at four places, two on the engine and two on the differential casing, a

When 2+2 really did add up to four: incredible luxury by the standards of early Ferrari 2+2s for the lucky occupants of the 365

Classical beauty to rival any two-seater: Pininfarina's body style spelled speed and balance in every carefully drawn line

configuration once again aimed at reducing the noise and vibration transmitted to the inside of the car.

The other innovation was the result of some careful collaboration between Ferrari and Koni, makers of the hydraulic dampers, to produce an efficient self-levelling system which would keep the rear suspension settings constant, whatever the loading on the back of the car. The self-levelling units were mounted behind the coil springs and controlled by sensors which detected suspension movements from the pre-determined settings. Hydraulic pressure which built up in the self-levelling units as the suspension flexed under road shocks was then used to force the suspension back to the correct setting.

One of the problems which was an inevitable consequence of the larger and more luxurious design of these four-seat production cars, was a big

Two outwardly identical production 365GTs of 1969 (opposite page, top). The one at the back is for Europe and that at the front for the USA, in the days when different markets didn't demand entirely different models . . .

Yet some changes were necessary: by 1968 the production car had lost its transparent headlamp (opposite page, bottom) in response to US laws

This shot of the 1967 version of the car (below) shows how little the basic body style changed over the years. Only the headlamp covers give its age away

increase in weight. And though the 365GT 2+2 looked similar to the 330GT 2+2 which it replaced (as well as showing a very discernible likeness to the Superfast), it was an appreciably heavier car. *Road & Track* tested one in 1969 and found it weighed in at only a fraction under two tons, ready for the road. This was the main reason why Ferrari found it necessary to fit power-assisted steering—fortunately, a carefully developed ZF system which took out some of the excess effort, but not all, leaving the driver with enough to do to convey the 'feel' of an earlier, totally unassisted Ferrari wheel.

Heavier the 365GT 2+2 may have been, but the 4 mm wider bores of the twelve cylinders, and the consequent increase in capacity of 423 cc over the 330 did provide an extra 20 bhp and a much larger increase in torque which went a long way to make up for the extra poundage. *Road & Track* went as far as to call the car 'The Queen Mother of Ferraris',

TWO TONS—AND 150 MPH

'The Queen Mother of Ferraris'. Seen from this angle, the imposing proportions of the 365GT 2+2 make it live up to Road & Track's *irreverent description of the model*

but they found room to add one or two kinder comments. The engine noise, they found, 'more remote and the exhaust more subdued than we've come to expect, but there's no question that it's a V12 with 24 valves working away'. They also noticed the 'usual Ferrari turbine-like smoothness, lack of temperament, and quiet idle with no fluffing of plugs every time you do a little slow driving'.

The weight penalty meant 'it isn't the hottest Ferrari we've ever tested, but it's no slouch either'. As proof, they covered the standing quarter mile in 15.2 seconds, with a top speed of 152 mph and acceleration times to 60 mph and 120 mph from a standing start in 7.2 seconds and 26.2 seconds respectively. On winding mountain roads 'or blasting past dawdlers, the five-speed gearbox is a delight with powerful synchromesh and reasonably light operation. The gearshift lever seems to be in just the right place too'.

How effective was the self-levelling rear suspension? 'This big 2+2 rides differently from any Ferrari we've driven. The large overhangs front and rear contribute to what we call a "level" ride with hardly a trace of pitching and that's good'. On the other hand, the testers reported 'a high degree of harshness' which helped to make the 365GT 2+2 'less of a rough-road car than lighter Ferraris'— nonetheless 'Out on the open road this car really comes into its own, as does any Ferrari: the power steering makes it seem light on its feet and the giant Michelin XVR tires furnish high cornering power with little fuss. Handling is close to neutral unless the tail is tweaked loose by power or by getting off the throttle: the former is recommended for making best time with the 2+2, and the latter brings out nothing abrupt or tricky'. Summing up, they assessed the new 2+2 as '. . . great . . . one man's expression of what a fast, roomy and luxurious car should be . . . it will do almost anything an

Two tons, a hundred and fifty miles per hour, power steering, and self-levelling independent rear suspension made the 365GT a VERY sophisticated motor car, even by Ferrari standards

The compact two-seat but confusing 365GTC: in just over a year almost 200 were made up to the beginning of 1970—but big changes killed it off in its prime

automobile would be asked to do: cruise at 150 mph, creep along in traffic, carry the wife and kids shopping or on a cross-country trip—all in air-conditioned comfort'.

As a statement of Ferrari's objectives in making

cars like the 365GT 2+2, this could hardly be improved on, and there were many more who agreed with the car's success in meeting them. In just over three years, from the end of 1967 until the beginning of 1971, more than eight hundred were made and sold, a figure which accounts for more than half of Ferrari's total production during that time. And when the car was replaced, it was not due to any falling off in its popularity, but rather to changes and improvements in other production models which made an updated version necessary.

During the time when the 365GT 2+2 was being made, other models with a similar pedigree were added to the assembly line. In the closing months of 1968, a 365GTS open two-seater took up the theme where the California had left off: this had the 4.4 litre engine in the short 240 cm wheelbase chassis, but with the independent rear suspension replacing the old rigid-axle set-up still used on the California. Production was small: only 20 or so cars were made, though this was itself an improvement on the 14 Californias which emerged from the shops. The 365GTC closed two-seat coupé appeared at the same time, with a similar pedigree, and though between 150 and 200 cars were made, it dropped out of production by the beginning of 1970, six months after the demise of the GTS. One of the reasons for both cars' short production life must have been the progressively increasing difficulty of meeting the legal requirements of the American market.

Simply meeting the safety requirements meant fearfully expensive crash-testing and modifications. Meeting the exhaust limits meant special ignition systems with extra valves and pumps to ensure complete combustion of gases leaving the cylinders, and all this was done for the 2+2. But rather than go through the same laborious process for the smaller-volume cars, Ferrari had something else entirely hidden up his sleeve.

Chapter 6
Four seats – four cams

Like their predecessors, the first whole generation of Ferrari 365 production cars had been powered by engines developed originally for racing Ferraris. So far, this had involved the classic V12 layout devized by Colombo and, occasionally, as modified by Lampredi—designs which, in their essentials, harked back to the late Forties and early Fifties. For engines like these to remain competitive in the forcing-house of international racing is an unrivalled tribute to the excellence of the original designs, but by the nineteen-sixties, changes were needed urgently.

They began in the 1965 racing season, when the 275P and 330P prototypes were given new V12s which, though the dimensions were unchanged, had new twin-cam heads on each cylinder bank, with each row of inclined valves being driven by one of the shafts without the need for rocker arms. These four-cam engines were fitted with fuel injection instead of carburettors, and had much more torque at lower speeds, with improved flexibility, as well as a welcome ten per cent boost in the peak power output—the 330P2 engine delivered 410 bhp compared with the 370 bhp of the 330P, and the 275P2 350 bhp compared with the 320 bhp of the original 275P of the season before.

By autumn of the following year, the four-cam version of the 3.3 litre engine made its appearance in a road car: the 275GTB/4, which graced the company stand at the Paris Show to begin its third year of production with the new power unit. In this version the engine had dry-sump lubrication, but reverted to carburettors, with no less than six double-choke Webers to keep its cylinders adequately supplied with fuel and air. With 300 bhp on tap in a relatively light and compact chassis, it provided fearsome performance in the right hands, as racing driver Jean-Pierre Beltoise proved when

The numberplate (or part of it) tells the story. This is the new 365 Ferrari, with the four-cam engine developed from the 1965 racing engines

The 365GT4 2+2 may have only an extra figure in its designation. But the 4 stood for four cams, and the new engine was matched by a completely new chassis

he tested it for the French magazine *L'Auto-Journal* and covered 46 miles of autoroute between the outskirts of Paris and Nemours on a Sunday afternoon in less than 23 minutes, an average of better than 121 mph '. . . in complete safety and in the greatest comfort, without once having to use the brakes hard and while carrying on a normal conversation with my passenger . . . which is remarkable enough without noting that I had to stop for the toll gates'.

The same four-cam and six Weber carburettor formula was later applied to the massive 81 by 71 mm 4.4 litre engine used in the 365 series of models,

but in this case the bigger bores forced a virtual redesign of the engine with longer cylinder blocks to allow adequate cooling spaces. This engine was used for the 365GTB/4 coupé and 365GTS/4 spider Daytona introduced in 1968—the coupé was later tested against no less an opponent than the mid-engined Lamborghini Miura, and the Ferrari not only proved to be 3 mph faster at 172 mph, but it outran the Miura in the standing start kilometre by just over two seconds.

Quite clearly, an engine which could deliver such shattering performance in compact coupés was bound to be equally useful in shifting the weight and size of more luxurious vehicles. And when, after a wait of eighteen months, the successor to the 365GT 2+2 emerged, in the shape of the 365GT4 2+2, it was virtually a new car in shape and design—a far more radical reform than the simple

The 365GT4 2+2 also marked the final break with the original Pininfarina design which had begun with the 250GTE so long before. The new shape was a lot lower, leaner and more businesslike than its predecessors had been

extra figure in the designation suggested. The new model, unveiled on the Ferrari stand at the Paris Motor Show of October 1972, looked quite unlike the earlier 365 2+2. And the chassis too was quite different.

In fact, the new 365 2+2's true parent was another four-cam car, a coupé which was itself the successor to the earlier 365GTC produced up to the

Because of changes in the mounting of engine and transmission, the seats were lower and the passenger compartment longer, giving rear seat passengers greater legroom and headroom than before

beginning of 1970. This was the 365GTC/4, which
appeared at the Geneva Show in the spring of 1971
with the 4.4 litre four-cam engine, as was already
being used in the Daytona, with six double-choke
Weber carburettors. But the difference was that
these Webers were not the traditional downdraught
type which had always been mounted in between
the cylinder banks of the Ferrari V12s. Instead, that

*At the same time, from the
driver's point of view, the
365GT4 2+2 was still every
inch a Ferrari . . .*

95

space on the new car was to be taken up with the various bits of anti-pollution equipment needed to satisfy the increasingly stringent requirements of the American market, so the carburettors were mounted horizontally on either side of the engine, feeding each cylinder bank through an inlet manifold set in between the twin camshafts.

This new arrangement produced a very useful reduction in overall height which allowed a lower bonnet line for the car. The chassis was made in a slightly different 250 cm wheelbase version, but because the seats, dashboard and controls were fitted further forward than before, there was still room behind them for a second pair of small seats, so that the car was in fact, if not in name, a 2+2— although the rear-seat passengers were not treated

The four-cam engine had the carburettors on the outside of the cylinder banks instead of in between them, allowing the car to have a much lower bonnet line

nearly as well as in the 365GT 2+2. On the other hand, the car did use the sophisticated self-levelling rear suspension developed for the previous 2+2 along with the front mounting for the gearbox, and the torque tube and four-point mounting for the engine-transmission package.

As a four-seater, the GTC4 may have been just pretending—*Road & Track* tested it in 1972, and referred to it as '. . . strictly a two-seater, its token rear seats folding to make a luggage area, but being available in case a child or two wants to ride along'. They went on to praise its mechanical smoothness 'Less mechanical thrash comes through from the engine room than in any previous Ferrari, and the controls are smoother and lighter than ever, making the car deliciously easy to drive well . . .

Seen from the front, the 365GT4 2+2's common ancestry with the other four-cam sports and racing cars is immediately apparent

Styling details: the individual lamps at the rear of the 365GT4 2+2, and the badge that tells it all . . .

there's just the right amount of purr from the four tail pipes, and when working hard in its upper rev range the engine sings the familiar and beautiful V12 song'.

In some ways, they found the straight-line performance disappointing: '. . . the GTC/4 will do only a mere 150 mph, and doesn't match even the old 330GTC in acceleration. But, as the Rolls-Royce man once said, it's adequate'. They also criticized 'a harsh, choppy low-speed ride which brings out some body squeaks', but, on the other hand 'It does smooth out at speed, just as if the car were a thoroughbred getting into its stride. The car is directionally stable at speeds up to its maximum. . . . Handling on winding roads is also excellent, with just the right sort of steering response and good adhesion, even in the rain . . .'

In sales terms, the GTC/4 showed the success of previous, more genuine four-seaters, in that five hundred were made in a year and a half, a production total which approached that of the highly successful Daytona during the same period, and which amounted to almost half Ferrari's total road-car production. The careful work which had been done on meeting the US controls had not been wasted either—most of the cars made went across the Atlantic, though this version was less powerful than the European model, which may have accounted for the testers' harsh words on the car's out-and-out performance.

Buyers who wanted a genuine four-seater had to wait a little longer, though. Until the autumn of 1972, in fact, when the 365GT4 2+2 arrived to take over. This used a chassis which was essentially that of the GTC (developed from the previous 2+2) but with the wheelbase stretched again to 270 cm, 5 cm longer than the original 365 2+2. This extra length was put to good use in improving the rear-seat accommodation over and above that of the GTC and even of the 2+2, although the car as a whole was actually 19 cm shorter, 4 cm lower and a centimetre wider than its predecessor.

The measurements only told part of the tale, however, for the car looked completely new. The greater room in the rear seats, together with the more generous legroom provided by the more spacious chassis, was matched by a new body shape which gave much-needed extra headroom too. This was arguably the first four-seater Ferrari which looked like a car for four people, even though its semi-saloon lines brought many enthusiasts to the verge of cardiac arrest as they sought for the right words to express their violent disapproval. Yet Pininfarina had produced a new body design of classic proportions, with a much larger window area and a low, sleek bonnet line made possible by electrically retracting headlamps and foglamps concealed behind the radiator grille and usable for daytime signalling. Though it looked light and graceful (by the standards of other four-seaters if not by those of other Ferraris), it was still a heavy car, weighing almost two tons in road trim. For all that, though, it could carry four people and their

One penalty of a lower bonnet line is the need for pop-up headlamps—these are the twin mountings of the 365GT4 2+2

Next page Like its predecessors, the sleek lines of the 365GT4 2+2 can best be appreciated from the side. The five-spoke alloy wheels, though handsome, represent another break with tradition

luggage in real comfort over long distances at speeds up to a genuine 150 mph in real Ferrari style.

Yet it's tempting to think of this car as something of a stopgap, for two reasons. It was a radical new design, in its arrangement and body shape if not in its mechanical parts, yet in four years of production, only 470 were made. Secondly, when the car was replaced, by the 400 series, its successor turned out to be virtually the same design with a larger engine and some subsequent modifications.

The reasons for the partial success of the car can be found in Ferrari's own marketing policy. American sales had always represented a large and vital part of his potential market, but increasingly tough legislation on safety and pollution requirements had created a situation where it was so complicated, time-consuming and expensive meeting all these regulations that it was virtually equivalent to making a completely new model. Ferrari's response to this was to drop plans for selling any more cars with the classic V12 engine in America. In future, he would concentrate on development of the 308 series for the US market. This had begun in 1973 with the Bertone-bodied 308GT4 based around a four-cam three-litre V8 with the cylinder banks set at 90 degrees, itself descended from a 1.5 litre Formula One engine of 1963. Here was a much newer engine, with much more long-term potential to justify the cost of the extra development work. From the early 1970s, the V12 would be kept for the smaller European market instead.

This was a momentous decision, in view of the part which the V12s of Colombo and Lampredi had played in the Ferrari story from the very beginning in the early days of peace during the 1940s and 50s. But it was far from the end of the story, for the Paris Show of October 1976 was to reveal a later, and larger version of the 365 engine, in the new Ferrari 400.

Chapter 7
The end of the line?

Summing up the differences between the 365GT4 2+2 and its successor is simple enough. The car which appeared for the first time on the company stand at the 1976 Paris Motor Show was labelled the Ferrari 400GT, but it looked almost exactly the same as its parent: the only details changed included the wheel mountings, the tail lights and the addition of a chin spoiler under the nose to improve airflow into the engine compartment. Under the skin, too, there were few enough alterations: the usual V12 had a longer stroke, at 77 mm, which increased the capacity from 4390 cc to 4823 cc without any alteration to the 81 mm bores. In fact, the engine was an almost square configuration, fed by six Webers and producing around 340 bhp at peak.

To anyone fortunate enough to be able to sit inside the car, there were more obvious alterations, however. The interior accommodation, and in particular the rear seats, were more lavish and luxurious than ever. Not only did the rear seat occupants enjoy more room than before, but there was the option of a second air-conditioning unit to keep them cool and comfortable as well. Leaving the seats at the end of the journey was made easier by an arrangement which slid the front seats forward to provide easier access whenever their backs were folded forward—and all four occupants were able to enjoy quadraphonic stereo in the hushed quiet of their luxury express.

In spite of the decades of steady development, this was still far enough away from the old Ferrari ideal to raise many eyebrows. But another change which made its presence felt in the driving compartment caused a much greater furore. For in one version of the car, the neat, short gearlever which had always been part of the furniture of every Ferrari was replaced by what many regarded as the ultimate heresy: the T-handle of an automatic transmission selector, a component which may have seemed at home on a Chevrolet or even a Rolls-Royce, but surely not on one of Enzo Ferrari's creations.

To Ferrari himself, there was nothing particularly sacred about the ideal of a manual gearbox.

The prototype 400GT, seen leaving the Maranello factory in 1976, shows the air dam below the grille, which improved airflow to the engine compartment

After all, his GT cars had taken on board air-conditioning and power steering, stereo and soft upholstery—why not automatics as well? An American Ferrari dealer had shown it was perfectly feasible in 1971 by fitting the General Motors' three-speed Turbo-Hydramatic system to his 365GT 2+2 (the same system was used by both Rolls-Royce and Jaguar) and sending the car to Ferrari for appraisal. Ferrari himself must have been impressed, because when the 400 Automatic made its first appearance, alongside its five-speed manual-gearbox 400GT stablemate, on the Paris Show stand, it used the self-same system to connect engine and wheels.

Enthusiasts' growls apart, how does the automatic fit in practice with the rest of the Ferrari prescription? According to David McKay of Australia's *Modern Motor* magazine, the works originally expected that 60 per cent of the 400s sold

The last straw for some Ferrari fanatics: the Paris Show and the 400A, the first production Ferrari to be fitted with an automatic gearbox . . .

would be the automatic version against 40 per cent manual—but that by 1978 more than 80 per cent of the cars ordered were automatics. Testing the automatic in the hurly-burly of the Paris rush-hour, he found that 'Unlike the manual five-speed model, which is only really suitable for open road motoring, where the driver dictates the gear changing rather than the traffic, the automatic Ferrari was instantly ready to leap forward into a hole in the streaming mass of cars at the merest touch of throttle. To have similar response in a manual, I would have been constantly in first or second slot and playing the clutch'.

Autocar too enjoyed their acquaintance with the

The right-hand-drive version of the 400A, which surprised and delighted some of its British road-testers . . .

automatic Ferrari, even in an article which also featured a test of the Berlinetta Boxer, from the very beginning 'The V12 engine springs to bubbling life as the quality sound of the starter motor dies away. Moving the automatic gearchange lever along its gate requires the detents to be overcome by mere gentle pressure from one's palm'.

But it was in the area traditionally meant for the sports Ferraris—out-and-out acceleration—that the automatic surprised both of the testers. *Autocar* again 'Full power acceleration in Low gear gives 60 mph at 6500 rpm, and gentle forward pressure eases the lever to the intermediate position and by the time 6500 rpm are up in this gear, the 400 is already doing over 100 mph. A confident push forward, without fear of going through to Neutral, has the car into Top gear and the relentless acceleration continues. Within five-eighths of a mile, you can be doing 130 mph and still the acceleration goes on, with 150 mph within its compass'.

Seen from the rear quarters, the 400 is a surprisingly elegant design. Another change is in the wheel fixings, with five studs replacing the knock-off hubs of the 356GT4 2+2

Far right Spot the *carburettors: the engine of the 400i, which replaced the traditional battery of Webers with a sophisticated fuel-injection system*

David McKay 'It's no big deal with screaming tyres and savage raw power, but a controlled rush at an unbelievable pace (unbelievable for such a large and luxurious conveyance) right up to the maximum of 240 kph (150 mph) and 6800 rpm. Acceleration times for the standing 400 metres and 1000 metres are 14.9 and 25.5 seconds respectively, with a

Very little to give away the automatic transmission from outside the car, apart from the tell-tale name tag. The three tail-lights on each side of the 365GT4 2+2 have given way to two

More opulence for the rear-seat passengers, with deeply padded upholstery, armrests and ashtrays

closing speed of 210 kph (132 mph) at the end of the kilometre. For those who believe that the five-speeder would eat the lethargic old automatic, they will be surprised to learn that the manual is only one-tenth quicker over the 400 metres and two-tenths over the kilo'.

Peter Dron of *Motor* was less sweeping in his praise, but admitted that 'the Ferrari's 0–60 mph time of 8.0 sec (100 mph is reached in 18.7 sec) is quick, but by no means outstanding in this class. But it is at over 100 mph when this machine comes into its own, and the engine seems to forget the fact that it's propelling nearly two tons of metal through the air'.

Sleek and purposeful and surprisingly compact, the 400i Automatic has come a long way from Ferrari's first four-seaters

With reactions like these, it's easy to forget how far the 400 has come from the original ideals which made road-going Ferraris such desirable prospects in the supercar league. When both manual and automatic 400s acquired fuel injection to become the 400i, in November 1979, it was another step in what *Car* magazine called taking 'the breed closer than it has ever been before to fulfilling the retiring, gentlemanly duties of a big Jaguar, Mercedes-Benz or BMW coupé. It is the practical Ferrari, the cosseting, comfortable, and to an extent the people-carrying Ferrari. It has easy cabin access, decent parking protection, an ornate interior, real boot space and it can be driven by those not abnormally long of arm or strong of left thigh'.

As a summing up of the 400i's virtues, that was a

Above right *Part of the control layout of the Ferrari 400—the gearlever reveals that this is one of the now increasingly rare manual-transmission models*

Above left *Still the most desirable driving seat in the world for millions of enthusiasts: the cockpit of the Ferrari 400 waiting for its lucky owner*

Above left *This, on the other hand, is the transmission control of the 400 Automatic. just like any other automatic, except in the results it produces . . .*

Above right *The 400 isn't normally exported to the United States, but a number have been modified, expensively, to meet the regulations. This one was photographed in Massachusetts in August 1982*

fair assessment. But in a sense it's a statement of another set of ideals, towards which the four-seat Ferraris have been striving ever since the days of the 250GTE 2+2. In truth, it isn't so much a dilution of the old sporting virtues as a process of providing performance in addition to space, comfort, sophistication and safety—in other words, not the final sacrifice of the classic qualities of the past, but the greatest success yet in combining those qualities in a more civilized and more efficient form of high-speed transport than anything even Ferrari had previously managed to produce.

Car and Driver came close to the truth when they described the 400i as 'a Ferrari for the guy who has cooled off enough about Ferraris that he no longer has to have a red one. This is a Ferrari for a man who wears suits'. And the fact that they were able to test-drive a model which is not even imported into the United States testified to its desirability—because the car they drove had had to be modified to meet the regulations at an extra cost of almost thirteen thousand dollars over and above the purchase price. One of a dozen or so in the whole country, 'which means you're not likely to meet yourself on the way down to the country club'. They summed it up as 'The one to have when you've had one of everything else'. They pointed out it has 'big doors, you can sit up straight inside, and it's not forever goading you to do something socially irresponsible'.

But there's more to the 400i than that. It's more than merely a splendid design in its own right, it's the last surviving heir to a great and historic

Simply add the mechanicals . . . the 400 body as it arrives from Pininfarina, painted and finished, with doors, windows and lights

The mechanicals being added . . . the 400 on the assembly line (if that's the right word for such a careful, and skilful, operation) at Maranello

tradition. As *Car and Driver* put it 'The 400i also happens to be the last Ferrari in production with a V12 engine. Maybe there will be another, maybe there won't, but all the other models now have flat twelves or V8s. And a Ferrari V12 is a magic engine, something every guy should own at least one of before the gas is all gone'.

Car summed up the whole ethos of this, the most interesting of all the four-seat Ferraris, contrasting its town-traffic manners with its behaviour on its own ground. In town, they said 'the car prowls about . . . the wheels thud into bumps in a way that would horrify the habitual Jaguar driver . . . the performance from standstill to traffic speed, say 40 mph, is only just sufficient to hold off a determinedly-driven Alfetta or Lancia Beta, because there is never a chance to use the rev band that contains the engine's serious power'.

But out on the open road, then 'the carping, if

that's what it sounded like, can stop abruptly . . .
under 25 mph the gearbox selects first with a
precise, hydraulically cushioned action. The car
lifts its nose and swallows road. The engine note is
suddenly the twelve-cylinder snarl-wail that has
been 34 years in the breeding . . . if you can register it
all quickly enough, you will note that at 45 mph the
rumble from the tyres is reduced by about half, and
that at 60 mph they absorb ripples truly smoothly
for the first time . . . the Ferrari breaks through a
barrier. Under that speed, it is simply a fat,
expensive, front-heavy luxurious car with an apparent potential for high performance. Above it—
and for the next 80 mph—it is absolutely the right
car for the job: grand touring'.

'At 5500 rpm and an indicated 94 mph, the
gearbox selects top . . . the transmission, apart from
a period of whine at 50 mph, is never heard. There is
only a smooth swish of wind past the windscreen
pillars, a continuing, rising bark from the engine
and a distant hum of tyres. At 120 mph, you start to
notice wind roar. If you've been listening to the
radio, you will have had to turn it up. At an
indicated 120–122 mph, 5000 rpm on the tachometer,
the car would be ready for an all-day cruise'.

As a statement of all that Enzo Ferrari had been
striving for in developing his production cars, this
would have been fine for the ending of a splendid
story. But the story hasn't finished yet: the 400i
remains in production for a fortunate few. And the
next thoroughbred in this brilliant family already
waits off-stage.

Chapter 8
Tomorrow's Ferrari?

For the whole of the Ferrari story, the name of Pininfarina has come at the top of the list of supporting players, designing the bodies of everything from track-burning prototypes to super luxury road cars. But this Farina family company has been around even longer than that: it started designing, and building car bodies at the beginning of the 1930s—which made 1980 its half-century, and a rather special anniversary to be commemorated in an ambitious, but very appropriate way.

They did it by doing what they have been doing for the last fifty years, by building a show car—but a very unusual, and very significant show car. Called the Pinin (for Pininfarina) it was essentially a sleek four-door saloon—but powered by the fearsome flat-12 Ferrari engine used in the Berlinetta Boxer, and crammed with interesting ideas. Aerodynamically, it was extremely efficient, with great care taken to eliminate all surface projections which might produce drag: a low bonnet line was made possible, not only by the flat configuration of the engine, but also by the use of specially developed headlamps with multiple reflectors which allowed them to be faired into the streamlined nose without needing to be retractable.

Inside, the keynote was comfort to a level beyond that previously offered to Ferrari owners—or their passengers. Even the rear seats had adjustable backs, and their were separate stereo systems for

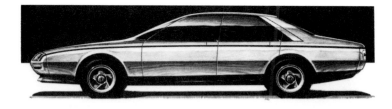

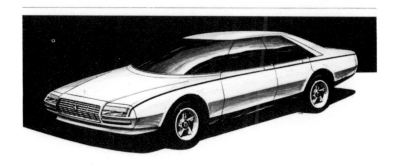

The shape of the future: initial sketches for the Pinin four-door saloon, based around the flat-12 engine of the Berlinetta Boxer

front and rear occupants. The electronic instrument panel is duplicated in the back to keep the passengers up-to-date. Warning lamps light up orange to show approaching problems, and red when things are serious—other displays warn when maintenance or replacements are due.

But the factor which makes the Pinin really stand out, even from the other ingenious and beautiful show cars turned out by companies like Pininfarina over the years, is that this is very likely to be the next four-seat Ferrari. Though the factory has steadfastly refused to commit itself to any decision in public, it's an open secret in the car world that plans exist for a production rate of three hundred cars a year from 1984 onwards, at a selling price of some £40,000 upwards. What isn't so clear, at least until the first production versions emerge from the workshops, is how much change will separate the show car from the showroom model.

At the moment, then, all that Ferrari fans have to go on is the 1980 Pinin show car. But if this is to be the pattern for the future, then it's hard to think of a better one. Of course, there will be hands upraised in horror at the four doors, just as there were in the past at four seats, or power steering, or automatic transmission. Of course a saloon as luxurious as this brings Ferrari into the Mercedes/Jaguar department in a way which previous production cars have never done quite so clearly. But with one

*Design sketch (*right*) shows Pininfarina's primary objective: more comfort than ever for rear-seat passengers. For the first time, their seats are identical with those in front*

*A link with the past (*below*): front end of Pinin prototype shows egg-crate radiator-grille similar to those of the first Ferrari bodies of the late Forties*

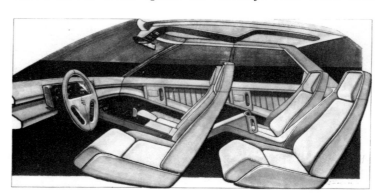

Above *Only the number of the cylinders and the mounting of the engine at the front of the car follow the Pinin's predecessors: for this is Ferrari's race-bred flat-twelve, power unit of the Berlinetta Boxer, also used to drive the Pinin*

Another ingenious feature of the Pinin (above left): the rear lights are cleverly concealed under glass tinted to match the body colour. Only when they light up (lower view) do they become apparent

important difference. *Car* magazine quoted a Ferrari dealer 'There are plenty of cars with leather interiors and marvellous carpets and seats, even space-age instrument graphics and facias, but if this new car goes and sounds like a Ferrari, there'll be more demand for it than they can cater for'.

Above *The Pinin making its first appearance, at the Turin Motor Show in the spring of 1980*

Right *The promise fulfilled: real four-door comfort, in the first four-door Ferrari, Pininfarina's ambitious and aerodynamic Pinin prototype*

Just about the only odd note in the styling is provided by the mesh radiator grille, a deliberate reminder of Pininfarina's first Ferrari body. It's a point worth making, for underneath all the sophistication, the new car—and its eventual successors—are still Ferraris. Its flat 12 engine has been proved, like all Ferrari engines, in the harsh, unforgiving, surroundings of the racing circuits, and its all-independently sprung chassis is developed from that of the 400i, itself descended from all the other

Futuristic lines shown by this rear view of the Pinin conceal a painstaking approach to detail which is intended to cut aerodynamic drag to the absolute minimum

121

models in our story. For whatever features the car may have—like the windows which overlap the door pillars to reduce wasteful turbulence, or the cleverly concealed bumpers which provide protection (and comply with legal requirements) without spoiling the line or creating drag—its most important attribute is the philosophy which made it possible at all. Enzo Ferrari's philosophy that everything else is secondary to performance—while his cars are safe, and reliable and comfortable, these are additional qualities to that single, most vital ingredient. That is what makes a Ferrari—any Ferrari—what it is. It is a quality possessed by all the cars we have looked at, but perhaps in its most tractable, most practical, most efficient and most usable form in this newest of Ferraris. Until the next one appears, and outdoes it.

The only Pinin so far built was a show prototype—but it could still well set the pace for the Ferraris of the late Eighties and early Nineties, a fitting conclusion to the 'Four-seat story' . . .

Appendix

Rather more than most cars, Ferraris have inspired those owners who can afford to pay for even more individuality by commissioning the top coachbuilders to go to work on their own personal versions of the Ferrari legend. Over the years, most of these cars have been based on the two-seat berlinette and spiders, but one or two have chosen a four-seater as material to work on. One of them was the elegant cabriolet built for Luigi Chinetti by Fantuzzi on the 250GTE 2+2 chassis and mechanicals, which was conspicuous for its broad roll-over bar behind the seats, similar to the racing prototypes. But this, though based on a four-seater, was rebuilt as a two-seater on completion in 1965.

It was Chinetti who commissioned all three of the special versions built on the 250GTE's successor, the 330GT 2+2. Two of them were by Michelotti, a vivid yellow and black cabriolet with, once again, a prominent rollbar behind the seats, and a coupé which bore a close family resemblance to it. The third special was an interesting estate car version by Vignale, shown at Turin in 1968, which was in fact the last design Vignale produced for Ferrari before Ghia took over his company a year later. This was an elegant design, marred only by the inevitable roll-bar, which had now expanded into a massive arch which overwhelmed the rest of the body.

Finally, the only known variation on the four-cam four-seaters (apart from standard convertibles with no basic restyling, and for once an exercise not sponsored by Chinetti: an unusual open-top version of the 365GT4 2+2 produced in 1975 by an ex-Ferrari engineer called Caliri and his Fly Studio. This featured, in addition to a transverse roll over bar which would have delighted Chinetti, a longitudinal bar stretching from the centre of the screen back to the centre of the transverse bar. The removable roof panels fitted on either side of this central rib, and the glass rear screen retracted electrically into the bodywork, leaving only the rear quarter panels which supported the overhead bars.

In this book, the story of the four-seat Ferraris has been told through the eyes of those who made the cars, those who put them on show, and those who bought them, tested them and enjoyed them when brand new and in peak condition. But what about those Ferrari fans who take on ownership today of one of the older cars—what kind of problems do

A highly effective disguise: few people looking at this lean and sporty creation by Carrozzeria Sports Cars of Modena would suspect that it is, in fact, based on the Ferrari 330GT . . .

they face in keeping it running and keeping the problems of age and wear, corrosion and damage at bay?

Probably the biggest obstacle to owning a Ferrari is not the purchase price—not in the case of second-hand models which have been with us for quite a while, at least. It so happens that the four-seaters, which were usually produced in larger numbers than many of the more exotic models, have depreciated further than their two-seat equivalents. But the prices for spare parts, and skilled attention, will be just as frightening for these cars as for any other Ferrari.

The costs can be divided very roughly into two kinds, the predictable and the completely unpredictable. Generally speaking, a Ferrari is most likely to suffer failures in two areas—the electrical system and the transmission, in either the clutch or the differential. This was confirmed in a survey among owners in America conducted by *Road & Track* in

. . . though the rear-end treatment of the design has worn rather less well, even by the standards of its time. (It was built in 1969)

1971: 17 per cent of Ferrari owners taking part mentioned these two areas. And though electrics have improved considerably in the more recent models, it's worth keeping a weather eye open when looking over a Ferrari as a buying prospect.

Obviously, as with any car, body rust—given our climate—is bound to be a major source of trouble. Earlier Ferraris, like many Italian cars, simply didn't have the anti-corrosion protection we've come to expect on lesser cars. On the other hand, not many Ferraris are driven to work every day on gritted roads in mid-winter. Engine problems, likewise, are not likely to come from neglect so much as over-enthusiasm: burned pistons due to fitting hotter plugs, collapsed exhaust systems (Ferrari exhaust prices can make the eyes of the unwary bulge with disbelief) from high speed running, distorted cylinder heads and blown gaskets from over-revving or overheating, and so on.

This is why engines rate the highest priority in buying—or restoring—any Ferrari. Wear of the valve stems and the soft valve guides is a common problem, and remember that a V12 has an awful lot of valves to be put right. The long-block Lampredi engines have problems of their own—though the cylinder liners are screwed into the heads to eliminate leaks at that end, they can leak through worn seals at the bottom instead. Loose timing chains can wear holes in the case, also letting oil and water mix, with disastrous results. And parts for these V12s are becoming almost impossible to get, making restoration doubly difficult.

Even when parts are obtainable, be prepared for big bills for engine attention. Replacing valves and rings can register a four-figure bill, while a complete engine overhaul can add another figure to that. There are only two real solutions to help cut the cost—do what one in four of *Road & Track*'s Ferrari owners do, and learn to carry out the maintenance yourself. Or follow Dean Batchelor's recommendation, and fit equivalent parts rather than factory originals, if they're too expensive. Some American owners now contemplate a home-grown V8 if a replacement Ferrari V12 is beyond the bounds of possibility—but is the resulting hybrid still a Ferrari?

The ingenious and effective open-top version of the 365GT4 2+2 by Fly Studio, designed and built in 1976

Specifications

Designation	Production	Cubic capacity	Wheelbase	Numbers built (approx.)
250GTE 2+2	1960–63	2953 cc	260 cm	950
330GT 2+2	1963–67	3967 cc	265 cm	1000
500 Superfast	1964–66	4962 cc	265 cm	37
365GT 2+2	1967–72	4390 cc	265 cm	800
365GT4 2+2	1972–76	4390 cc	270 cm	470
400GT & i	1976 on	4823 cc	270 cm	Still in
400 Auto	1976 on	4823 cc	270 cm	production
Pinin	1980	4943 cc	275 cm	Prototype only

250GTE 2+2

Engine—type: 60 degree V12. Bore & stroke 73 × 58.8 mm/2.87 × 2.315 in. Displacement 2953 cc/180 cu. in. Compression ratio 8.8:1. Bhp 240 @ 7000 rpm (approx.). Single overhead camshaft for each bank. Roller cam followers. Three Weber twin choke 40DCL/6, downdraught **Transmission** Four speed, all synchromesh. Overdrive fifth. Single dry plate clutch. 4.57 or 4.25:1 axle ratio **Suspension** front: independent with unequal length wishbones, coil springs and telescopic shock absorbers. Rear: Live axle with semi-elliptic springs, parallel trailing arms, telescopic shock absorbers **Chassis** Tubular steel, welded ladder type. **Brakes, wheels, tyres** Four wheel discs, centre lock Borrani wire, 6.50×15 front and rear tyres **Dimensions** Wheelbase 2600 mm/102.3 in., front track 1354 mm/53.3 in., rear track 1394 mm/54.9 in. **Chassis numbers** 2043GT to 4961GT, approximately 950 built. Approximately 50 cars, 4963GT to 5176Gt, were built with the 330 engine

330GT 2+2

Engine type: 60 degree V12. Bore & stroke 77 × 71 mm/3.03 × 2.79 in. Displacement 3967 cc/242 cu. in. Compression ratio 8.8:1. Bhp 300 @ 6600 rpm (approx.) Single overhead camshaft for each bank. Roller cam followers.
Three Weber twin choke 40DCZ/6, downdraught

Transmission Four speed, all synchromesh. Electrically operated overdrive 'fifth'. Late 1966–67 cars used a five speed gearbox. Single dry plate clutch. 4.25:1 axle ratio

Suspension front: independent with unequal length wishbones, coil springs and telescopic shock absorbers. Rear: live axle with semi-elliptic springs, parallel trailing arms, telescopic shock absorbers

Chassis Tubular steel, welded ladder type

Brakes, wheels, tyres Four wheel discs, centre lock Borrani wire to 1965 then cast alloy wheels as standard and wire as option, 205 × 15 front and rear tyres

Dimensions Wheelbase 2650 mm/104.2 in., front track 1397 mm/55.2 in., rear track 1389 mm/54.7 in.

Chassis numbers 5165 GT to 10193GT, approximately 1000 built.

Approximately 50 cars, 4963GT to 5175GT, with 250GTE bodywork were built using the 330GT engine

500 Superfast

Engine type: 60 degree V12. Bore & stroke 88 × 68 mm/3.46 × 2.68 in. Displacement 4962 cc/302.7 cu. in. Compression ratio 8.8:1. Bhp 400 @ 6500 rpm (approx.). Single overhead camshaft for each bank. Roller cam followers.

Three Weber twin choke 40DCZ/6, downdraught

Transmission Five speed, all synchromesh. Four speed plus overdrive was used in 1964 and on some early 1965 cars. Multi-plate clutch. 10 plus axle ratios were available from 410 and 400 SuperAmerica and 365GT 2+2

Suspension front: independent with unequal length wishbones, coil springs and telescopic shock absorbers. Rear: live axle with semi-elliptic springs, parallel trailing arms, telescopic shock absorbers

Chassis Tubular steel, welded ladder type

Brakes, wheels, tyres Four wheel discs, centre lock Borrani wire, 6.50 × 16 tyres front and rear

Dimensions Wheelbase 2650 mm/104.2 in., front track 1407 mm/55.5 in., rear track 1397 mm/55.2 in.

Chassis numbers 5951SF to 8897SF, approximately 37 built

365GT 2+2

Engine type: 60 degree V12. Bore & stroke 81 × 71 mm/3.19 × 2.79 in. Displacement 4390 cc/268 cu. in. Compression ratio 8.8:1. Bhp 320 @ 6600 rpm (approx.). Single overhead camshaft for each bank. Roller cam followers.

Three Weber twin choke 40DFI/5, downdraught

Transmission Five speed, all synchromesh. Single dry plate clutch. 4.25:1 axle ratio

Suspension front: independent with unequal length wishbones, coil springs and telescopic shock absorbers. Rear: independent with unequal length wishbones, coil springs and telescopic shock absorbers. Hydro-pneumatic levelling

Chassis Tubular steel, welded ladder type

Brakes, wheels, tyres Four wheel discs, Cromadora cast alloy with Borrani wire optional, 215/70VR×15 tyres front and rear

Dimensions Wheelbase 2650 mm/104.2 in., front track 1437 mm/56.6 in., rear track 1468 mm/75.8 in.

Chassis numbers 10791GT to 14099GT, approximately 800 built

365GT4 2+2

Engine Type: 60 degree V12. Bore & stroke 81×71 mm/3.19×2.79 in. Displacement 4390 cc/268 cu. in. Compression ratio 8.8:1. Bhp 320@ 6200 rpm (approx.). Twin overhead camshafts for each bank. Six Weber twin choke 38DCOE59/60, sidedraught

Transmission Five speed, all synchromesh. Single dry plate clutch. 4.09:1 axle ratio

Suspension front: independent with unequal length wishbones, coil springs and telescopic shock absorbers, anti-roll bar. Rear: independent with unequal length wishbones, coil springs and telescopic shock absorbers, anti-roll bar

Chassis Tubular steel

Brakes, wheels, tyres Four wheel discs, Cromadora cast alloy, 215/70VR×15 front and rear tyres

Dimensions 2700 mm/106.3 in., front track 1470 mm/57.9 in., rear track 1500 mm/59 in.

Chassis numbers 17121 to . . .

400GT, i, Automatic,

Engine Type: 60 degree V12. Bore & stroke 81×77 mm/3.19×3.05 in. Displacement 4823 cc/294 cu. in. Compression ratio 8.8:1. Bhp 340 @ 6500 rpm (approx.). Twin overhead camshafts for each bank. Six Weber 38DCOE110/111, sidedraught for early cars, Bosch K-Jetronic for cars with 'i' suffix

Transmission Manual: five speed, all synchromesh. Automatic; GM Turbo 400 3-speed gearbox. Single dry plate clutch for manual. 4.3:1 axle ratio for manual, 3.25:1 for automatic.

Pinin

Suspension front: independent with unequal length wishbones, coil springs and telescopic shock absorbers, anti-roll bar. Rear: independent with unequal length wishbones, coil springs and telescopic shock absorbers, anti-roll bar
Brakes, wheels, tyres Four wheel discs, Cromadora cast alloy wheels, 215/70VR × 15 front and rear tyres
Dimensions 2700 mm/106.3 in., front track 1470 mm/57.9 in., rear track 1500 mm/59 in.
Chassis numbers 27001 and still in production
Engine type: flat 12, as fitted to 512BB. Bore & stroke 82 × 78 mm/3.23 × 3.07 in. Displacement 4943 cc/302 cu. in. Compression ratio 9.2:1 (approx.), Bhp 360 @ 6800 rpm (approx.).
Twin overhead camshafts for each bank
Dimensions Wheelbase 2750 mm/108.3 in., front track 1540 mm/60.6 in., rear track 1540 mm/60.6 in.

Acknowledgements

By its very complexity Ferrari history needs to draw material from a multitude of sources. For this book photographs arrived from all over Europe, North America and other far flung outposts. All was co-ordinated in two places, and then finally brought together in London. Jonathan Thompson did all the work in the USA and Mirco Decet completed it in London. Thank you both.

Many others helped along the way. Thanks are due to the following; Dott. Mateoni at Ferrari Esercizio Fabbriche Automobili e Corse SpA in Modena; Dott. Calmassa of Industrie Pininfarina SpA in Turin; Mark Konig of Maranello Concessionaires Ltd in Egham; Modena Engineering Ltd at East Horsley; Sussex Sports Cars at Forest Row and Godfrey Eaton of the British end of the Ferrari Owners Club.

Photographs came from the following; Dr Seifert, Image PR Ltd, the late Peter Coltrin, *Motor Trend*, Alessandro Stefanini, Bob Tronolone, *Inter Auto*, Studio Moisio, Bernard Cahier, Dean Batchelor and *Auto Italiana*.

Index